COWBOYS

© Aladdin Books Ltd 2009

Designed and produced by
Aladdin Books Ltd
PO Box 53987
London SW15 2SF

First published in 2009
by Franklin Watts
338 Euston Road
London NW1 3BH

Franklin Watts Australia
Level 17/207 Kent Street
Sydney NSW 2000

A catalogue record for
this book is available
from the British Library.

Dewey Classification:
973.5

ISBN 978 0 7496 8642 0

Franklin Watts is a division of
Hachette Children's Books,
an Hachette Livre UK company.
www.hachettelivre.co.uk

Illustrators
Susanna Addario, Alessandro Baldanzi, Francesca
D'Ottavi, Paola Ravaglia, Roberto Simone – McRae
Books, Florence, Italy

TRUE STORIES AND LEGENDS

COWBOYS

Jim Pipe

Aladdin/Watts
London • Sydney

Contents

INTRODUCTION

Cowboys are cattle herders that ride horses. There have been cowboys all over the world for hundreds of years, but the most famous cowboys lived in the American West over 100 years ago. In movies, these cowboys are shown as heroes, outlaws, gamblers and gunfighters. Real cowboys were all of these things, but it can be hard to tell the true stories from the legends.

Cowboys were hired hands. They spent most of their time looking after cattle – herding them, rounding them up and driving them to market. Though they enjoyed riding and the outdoor life, it was very hard work and they were poorly paid.

This book looks at cowboys (and cowgirls) and the rough Old West they lived in – a world of trails, ranches, saloons and the open prairies.

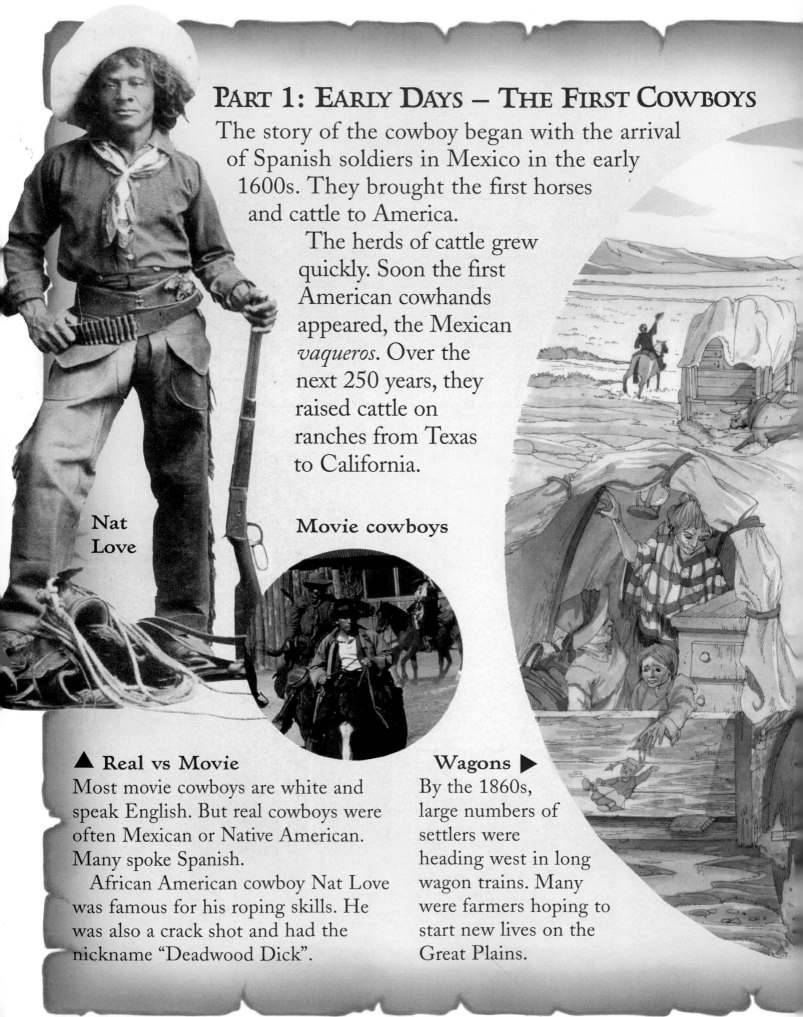

PART 1: EARLY DAYS – THE FIRST COWBOYS

The story of the cowboy began with the arrival of Spanish soldiers in Mexico in the early 1600s. They brought the first horses and cattle to America.

The herds of cattle grew quickly. Soon the first American cowhands appeared, the Mexican *vaqueros*. Over the next 250 years, they raised cattle on ranches from Texas to California.

Nat Love

Movie cowboys

▲ Real vs Movie

Most movie cowboys are white and speak English. But real cowboys were often Mexican or Native American. Many spoke Spanish.

African American cowboy Nat Love was famous for his roping skills. He was also a crack shot and had the nickname "Deadwood Dick".

Wagons ▶

By the 1860s, large numbers of settlers were heading west in long wagon trains. Many were farmers hoping to start new lives on the Great Plains.

◀ **Abraham Lincoln** became President in 1861. To end slavery in America, he led the Union (the northern states) in a war against the South. By 1863, slavery was abolished.

The Cowboy Era ▼

Texan cowboys learned from Mexican *vaqueros* how to raise and herd cattle. When the Civil War ended in 1865, they led the great cattle drives from Texas to the cities in the North.

They were joined by thousands of ex-soldiers from the North who had no job at the end of the war. Slaves who had fought for the North also became cowboys when they gained their freedom.

Soldiers leave the Union Army.

THE GOLDEN AGE OF COWBOYS

During the Civil War, thousands of cattle were left to run wild in Texas. When the war ended, ranch owners realised they could sell these cattle for a good price in the North. Businessman J.G. McCoy arranged for a railway to be built from Kansas City to the town of Abilene. From there, the cattle could be shipped to Chicago.

The journey from Texas to the rail stations was known as the "long drive". It was over 1500 km long. During the 1870s and 1880s, cowboys were hired to round up and drive cattle slowly north across the Great Plains.

The Great Cattle Trails

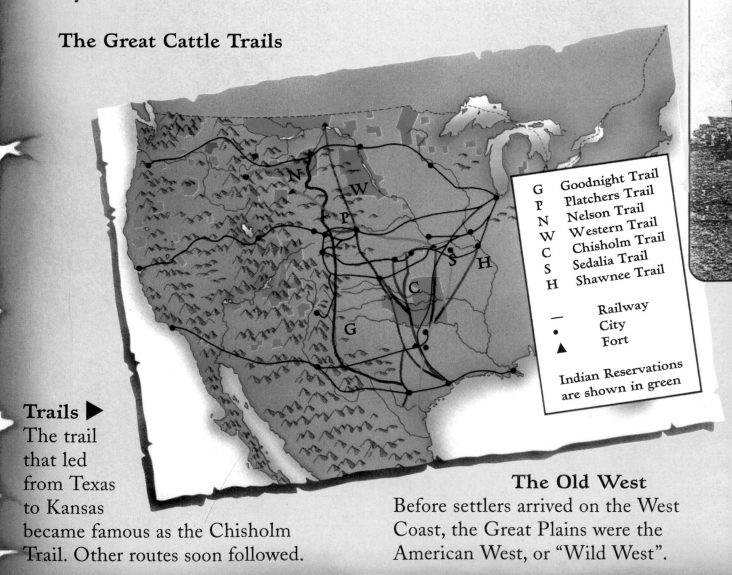

G	Goodnight Trail
P	Platchers Trail
N	Nelson Trail
W	Western Trail
C	Chisholm Trail
S	Sedalia Trail
H	Shawnee Trail

— Railway

• City

▲ Fort

Indian Reservations are shown in green

Trails ▶
The trail that led from Texas to Kansas became famous as the Chisholm Trail. Other routes soon followed.

The Old West
Before settlers arrived on the West Coast, the Great Plains were the American West, or "Wild West".

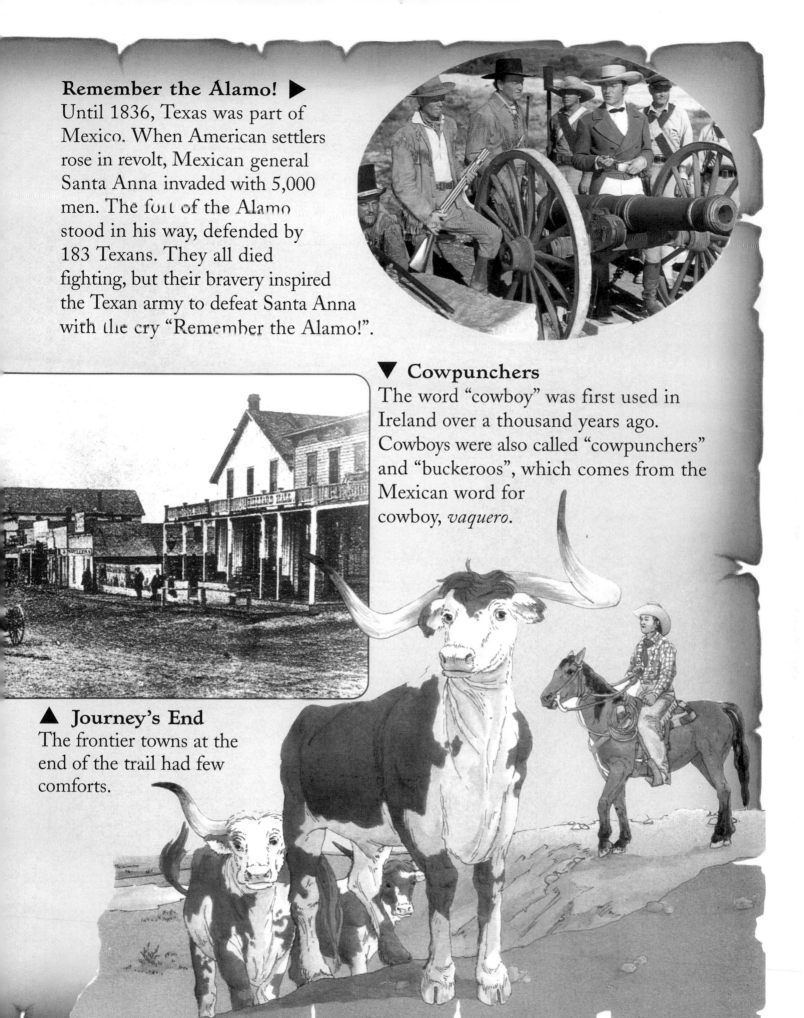

Remember the Alamo! ▶
Until 1836, Texas was part of
Mexico. When American settlers
rose in revolt, Mexican general
Santa Anna invaded with 5,000
men. The fort of the Alamo
stood in his way, defended by
183 Texans. They all died
fighting, but their bravery inspired
the Texan army to defeat Santa Anna
with the cry "Remember the Alamo!".

▼ **Cowpunchers**
The word "cowboy" was first used in
Ireland over a thousand years ago.
Cowboys were also called "cowpunchers"
and "buckeroos", which comes from the
Mexican word for
cowboy, *vaquero*.

▲ **Journey's End**
The frontier towns at the
end of the trail had few
comforts.

PART 2: COWBOY LIFE – THE TRAIL DRIVE

The "long drive" began with a round-up. Young calves and strays, called "mavericks", were branded with the ranch owner's mark. A herd of up to 5,000 cattle were chosen. A herd this size needed 12 cowboys plus the trail "boss", the cook and a wrangler.

Then the cowboys set out on their long journey northward, easing the huge herd across rocky scrubland, flooded rivers and scorching deserts.

◀ Cattle Kingdom

In the 1870s, the Plains were a "Cattle Kingdom" run by businessmen who made huge fortunes from the cattle trade. Cattle baron Charles Goodnight owned 100,000 head of cattle and over 5,000 square km of Texas land.

Remuda

Trail Teamwork

The trail "boss" rode next to the leaders of the herd. "Swing" and "flank" riders rode at the sides, while the "drags" rode at the back in a cloud of dust. A wrangler looked after the spare horses, the *remuda*.

Refrigeration

At the end of the trail, cattle were herded onto trains and shipped to the big cities in the east and north to be sold for meat.

When Gustavus Swift invented the refrigerated meat wagon in 1881, there was no longer any need to move live animals.

▲ **The Chuck Wagon**

The first to leave the round-up was the chuck wagon, driven by the cook, or "grub-slinger". This carried the food stores, cooking equipment, bedding and spare saddles. "Chuck" was cowboy slang for food, which was usually a plate of "sowbelly" (pork), bread and beans. Wild animals shot for the pot, such as jackrabbits, also made a tasty stew.

▲ **River Crossing**

Cattle fear water. If they panic while crossing a river, they can drown themselves and any cowboys nearby. After heavy rains, rivers can also sweep cattle downstream.

THE BIG FOUR

Brand Book

OIL

A COWBOY'S BEST FRIEND

A cowboy needed a good horse for his job. Horses, or "broncos", were allowed to run wild for two years. Then a "bronco-buster" tamed them, so they were safe to ride. After capturing a bronco, he put a saddle on its back. He clung on while the horse bucked. Slowly, it got used to being ridden.

Some cowboys owned their own horse, but most used horses supplied by the ranch – up to six a day. The best horses were fast, agile and steady on their feet. They were used to "cut", or separate, unbranded calves from their mothers.

A **cowboy** with a well-trained horse could ride 15 hours a day. Some cowboys rode so much they walked bow-legged!

Cowboy on horseback

Horn

Seat

Cantle

Skirt

Fender

Ties

Stirrup

◀ **Saddle**
A good saddle cost 10 months' salary but could last 30 years. It was made of wood and metal covered with leather.

The horn was used to hold the end of a rope when a cowboy was lassoing a calf. Long stirrups allowed a cowboy to mount the horse quickly, while a fender protected his legs against a horse's sweat.

A **bandanna** shielded a cowboy's face from dust.

▲ A **felt hat** had a wide brim that kept the Sun and rain off a cowboy's face.

▼ **Cowboy clothes** were comfortable but tough. After a day on the trail, cowboys would have looked dusty and ragged compared to the neat cowboys in this old movie.

Spurs were spiked wheels worn on the heel. They were used to prick a horse to make it ◄ go faster.

Long johns

Chaps

Johns, Chaps and Boots ►
Under their shirt and woollen trousers, cowboys wore one-piece underwear called "long johns". They wore leather or fur chaps (say "shaps") to protect their legs from thorns and frost. Their leather boots had high heels to keep their feet in the stirrups – and to make them look tall!

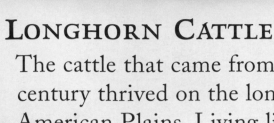

LONGHORN CATTLE

The cattle that came from Spain in the 16th century thrived on the long buffalo grass of the American Plains. Living like wild animals, they became fast, long-legged and tough. Their giant horns, up to 2 metres wide, gave them the name "Longhorn".

Herding Longhorns was dangerous as they were "ornery", or bad-tempered. A Longhorn weighed 400 kilograms, but its meat was often tough. By the 1870s, Longhorns were already being replaced by gentler breeds that produced better beef.

Stampede! ▶
Longhorns were so wild it didn't take much to spook them. A sudden noise such as a gunshot or a crack of lightning could set the whole herd off in a mad stampede.

Stampedes were especially dangerous at night. A cowboy on foot could be trampled by thousands of pounding feet. On stormy nights, cowboys often slept fully-clothed with their horses ready nearby.

▼ New Breeds
The Aberdeen Angus and the Hereford were brought from England to replace the Longhorn.

Longhorn **Shorthorn** **Aberdeen Angus** **Hereford**

Branding ▼

During the round-up each year, all the new calves were branded: the owner's mark was burned into the skin with a red-hot iron. One cowboy on horseback "cut" the calf from its mother, then lassoed it. The calf was then wrestled to the ground and dragged toward a fire where it was branded.

Ropes

Cowboys became experts at using a flying loop, or lasso, to catch Longhorn cattle on the open ranges.

A full rope was around 10 m long and was made of twisted cowhide or hemp.

Famous brands

Buffalo hide

THE BUFFALO

The Longhorn shared the Great Plains
with millions of buffalo. Some herds were so
big it took a day to ride past them! But the
cattle barons wanted to get rid of these
majestic animals to make way for cattle. Traders
paid well for the buffalo hides which made good leather.

In the 1870s, hunters were encouraged onto the Plains.
A mass slaughter began. Soon, nothing
remained of the giant herds except piles
of bones. By 1883, just 1,500 buffalo
were left alive out of tens of millions.

▼ In 1894, **buffalo** were protected by law. Today
there are over 200,000 buffalo in North America.

Slaughter
An adult buffalo weighs almost a
tonne so it has no natural enemies.
When attacked, it stands still in a
group – an easy target for a hunter.
Armed with the new Sharps rifle, one
man could kill 250 buffalo in a day.

Blood Sport ▶
Some sportsmen
travelled to the hunt by
train. Hunters skinned the
dead buffalo, then left their
bodies to rot. Some cut out the
tongue to be eaten as a delicacy.

Native Americans living on the ▶ Plains used the buffalo for food, clothing and shelter. Once the buffalo herds were destroyed, many tribes were forced to leave – or starve.

Wild Bill Hickok

Buffalo Hunter
In 1867, William Cody ("Buffalo Bill") killed 5,000 buffalo in less than 18 months to feed men working on the railways. By the 1880s, 5,000 hunters and skinners were at work, including famous names such as Wyatt Earp and Wild Bill Hickok.

Following the Herd
Many cowboys became buffalo hunters. Hunting buffalo was an easy way to make a living compared to the long drive.

Buffalo hunt

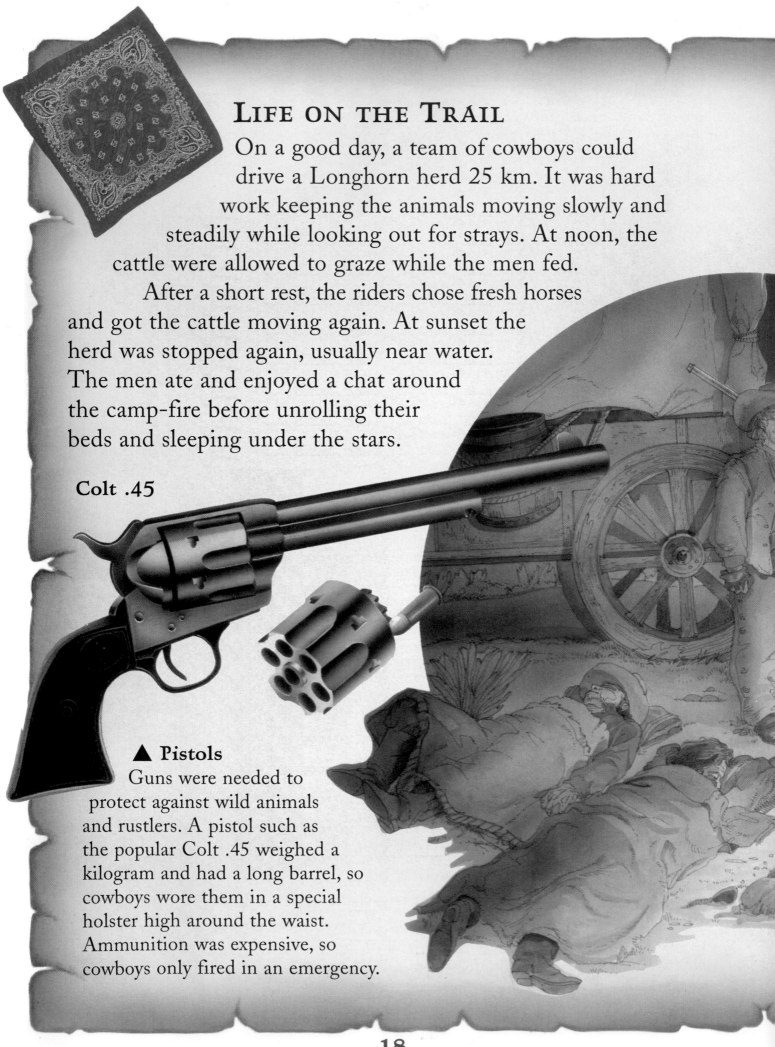

LIFE ON THE TRAIL

On a good day, a team of cowboys could drive a Longhorn herd 25 km. It was hard work keeping the animals moving slowly and steadily while looking out for strays. At noon, the cattle were allowed to graze while the men fed.

After a short rest, the riders chose fresh horses and got the cattle moving again. At sunset the herd was stopped again, usually near water. The men ate and enjoyed a chat around the camp-fire before unrolling their beds and sleeping under the stars.

Colt .45

▲ Pistols
Guns were needed to protect against wild animals and rustlers. A pistol such as the popular Colt .45 weighed a kilogram and had a long barrel, so cowboys wore them in a special holster high around the waist. Ammunition was expensive, so cowboys only fired in an emergency.

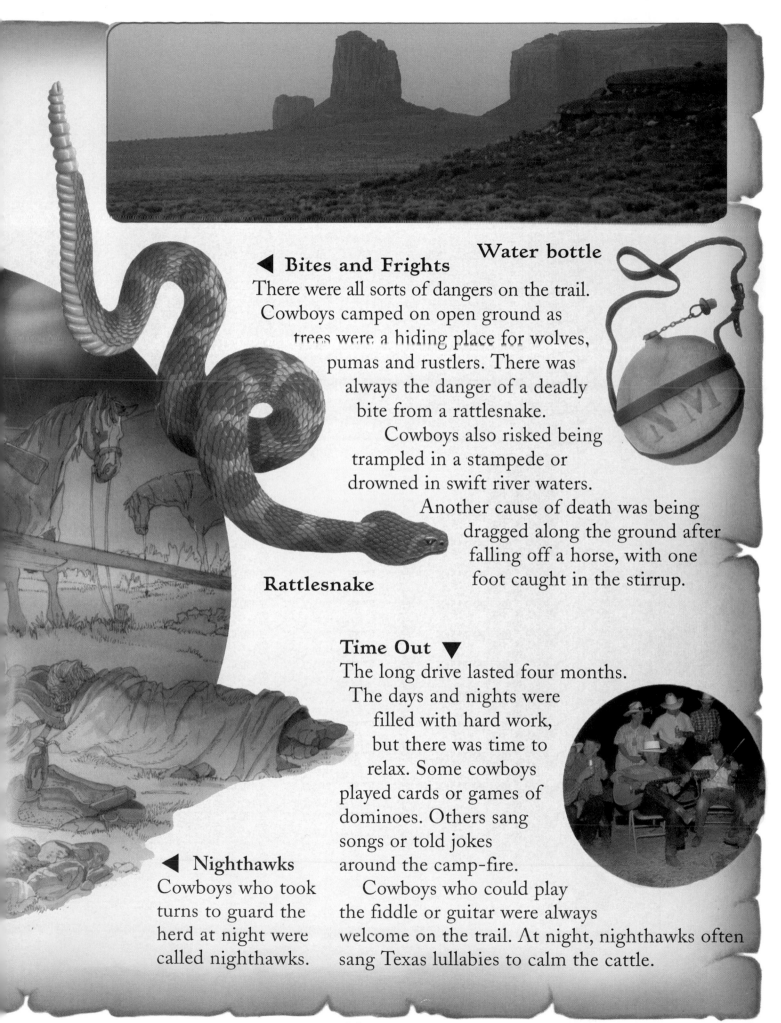

◄ Bites and Frights

Water bottle

There were all sorts of dangers on the trail. Cowboys camped on open ground as trees were a hiding place for wolves, pumas and rustlers. There was always the danger of a deadly bite from a rattlesnake.

Cowboys also risked being trampled in a stampede or drowned in swift river waters.

Another cause of death was being dragged along the ground after falling off a horse, with one foot caught in the stirrup.

Rattlesnake

Time Out ▼

The long drive lasted four months. The days and nights were filled with hard work, but there was time to relax. Some cowboys played cards or games of dominoes. Others sang songs or told jokes around the camp-fire.

◄ Nighthawks

Cowboys who took turns to guard the herd at night were called nighthawks.

Cowboys who could play the fiddle or guitar were always welcome on the trail. At night, nighthawks often sang Texas lullabies to calm the cattle.

PART 3: WILD WEST – COWTOWNS

Once they reached the cowtowns at the end of the trail, the cowboys stayed with the herd until the cattle had been driven into pens and sold. Then it was time to be paid – up to $100 in one sum. This didn't last long!

First up, was a shave and a good soak in a bath to wash off weeks of dust and sweat. Then it was off to the store for a new set of clothes before heading to the saloon. Here, cowboys could get a hearty meal, a few drinks and perhaps a dance or two. Soon, however, it was time to head south for the next round-up.

▼ Spittin' Tobacco

Many cowboys chewed tobacco, so every saloon had a spittoon for them to spit into when their 'baccy had lost its taste. As lazy cowboys often missed the spittoon, sawdust was sprinkled on the floor to soak up the mess.

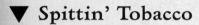

Spittoon

Saloon

Bawdy house

20

▲ Prairie nymphs lived tough lives, unlike the very glamourous women that appear in many old cowboy movies.

Gambling

Big Nose Kate ▶
It was a lonely life on the trail. At the end of a drive, cowboys were eager to find some female company. "Prairie nymphs", such as Big Nose Kate and Squirrel-tooth Alice, made a living entertaining cowboys.

The bawdy houses they worked in were usually more comfortable than saloons. Here cowboys danced to music played on a piano or fiddle.

Shoot Outs
The mix of drink and gambling in saloons often led to fights. But there were few shoot outs of the kind seen in the movies. In many towns, cowboys were ordered to hang up their guns before they entered a saloon.

WOMEN OF THE WILD WEST

Women worked alongside men on ranches all over the West – in an age when they were expected to stay at home wearing long dresses and working around the house.

Some women managed ranches while their husbands were away. Few joined the long drive, as any woman wearing trousers and riding like a man risked being put in gaol. Belle Star and "Cattle Annie" became cattle thieves and joined outlaw gangs. By the 1880s, other women were performing in Wild West shows as rodeo riders.

▲ "Calamity" Jane was born Martha Jane Canary. She wore men's clothing, chewed tobacco and was handy with a gun.

"Cattle Annie" and "Little Britches"

To the Rescue!
"Calamity" Jane tried all sorts of jobs before becoming a scout for the army. She got her nickname after rescuing her captain in an ambush. She also saved six passengers when their stagecoach was attacked by Sioux warriors. Later, "Calamity" appeared in Buffalo Bill's Wild West Show as a rider and trick shooter.

Belle Starr

Known as the "Bandit Queen", Belle Starr came from a wealthy family but chose a life of robbing stagecoaches and stealing cattle.

Belle was a skilled rider who could handle a gun and was friends with the notorious outlaw Jesse James. One night, as Belle was riding home, she was shot dead, perhaps by one of her own gang.

Belle Star

In the Movies

The women in cowboy movies are usually prairie nymphs or pretty farmers' wives.

Few films show how tough and dangerous life really was for most women in the Wild West.

"Cattle Annie" and "Little Britches"

Annie McDougal and Jennie Stevens were teenagers when they joined the Doolin gang in 1893. Soon they were famous for rustling cattle and robbing trains as "Cattle Annie" and "Little Britches" (Jennie wore men's clothes). When the law finally caught up with the two girl bandits, they fought like wildcats. After two years in prison, both gave up their life of crime.

THE LAWMEN

In the early days of the American West, there were few towns well run enough to have their own lawmen. Everything changed with the cattle boom.

Rowdy cowboys let off steam by riding into town and firing their pistols into the air – others got into fights over card games. Soon, many towns had their own sheriff who could round up a posse of townsmen to help him arrest lawbreakers. Cattle towns were wild places, but most cowboys didn't rob banks or steal cattle.

▲ Winchester Rifle

Pistols were only useful at short range, so many cowboys carried a rifle such as the popular Winchester '73, which was known as the "gun that won the West".

Wyatt Earp

A Wild West town

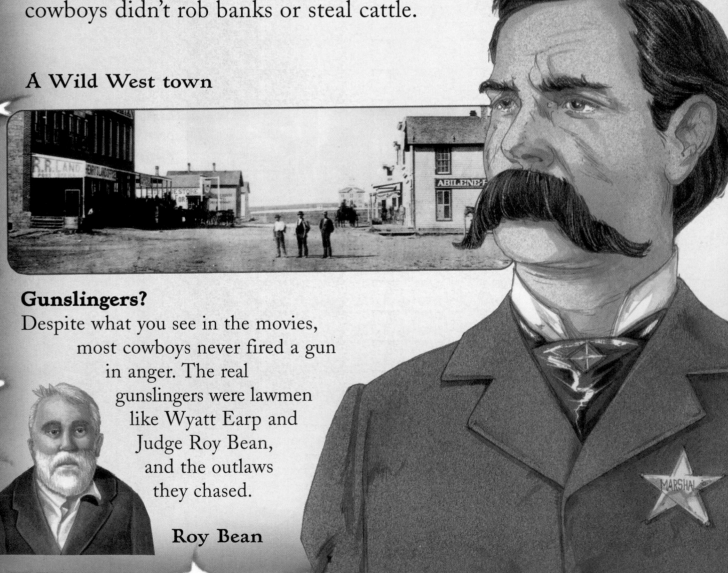

Gunslingers?

Despite what you see in the movies, most cowboys never fired a gun in anger. The real gunslingers were lawmen like Wyatt Earp and Judge Roy Bean, and the outlaws they chased.

Roy Bean

Winchester '73

Badges ▼

Lawmen dressed like most other people so they wore a badge to show who they were. Sheriffs and their assistants, called deputies, wore a "tin star".

Marshals, who worked for the US government and had power over a wide area, wore a shield.

Murder at the OK Corral ▼

In the movies, Virgil and Wyatt Earp and "Doc" Holliday are brave lawmen who fight the dangerous Clanton gang in a dramatic shoot out.

In reality, the Earps were the town bullies and cold-blooded killers. They were looking for trouble. Two of the men they shot weren't even carrying a gun.

▲ The Posse

A sheriff couldn't stop a gang of outlaws or rustlers on his own. Luckily, local citizens were often willing to become part-time lawmen. They joined a search party, or posse, to help the sheriff capture the outlaws – dead or alive!

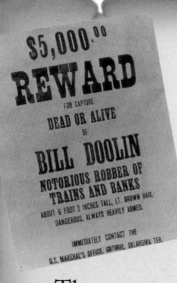

$5,000.00
REWARD
FOR CAPTURE
DEAD OR ALIVE
OF
BILL DOOLIN
NOTORIOUS ROBBER OF
TRAINS AND BANKS
ABOUT 6 FOOT 2 INCHES TALL, LT. BROWN HAIR,
DANGEROUS, ALWAYS HEAVILY ARMED.
IMMEDIATELY CONTACT THE
U.S. MARSHAL'S OFFICE, GUTHRIE, OKLAHOMA TER.

OUTLAWS

Lawmen often found it hard to catch criminals in the wide open spaces of the Old West. So they posted "Wanted – Dead or Alive" notices, making the criminals outlaws.

Billy the Kid

These men were now outside the law, so anyone could capture or kill them.

Most outlaws were violent cattle rustlers, bank or stagecoach robbers and murderers. Yet Jesse James and Butch Cassidy became heroes, thanks to the many books and songs that were written about them.

The Teenage Outlaw ▶

William H. Bonney, nicknamed "Billy the Kid", killed his first man at the age of 12. He then fled to New Mexico where he later led a band of cattle rustlers.

Billy killed at least 27 people and though he was captured and sentenced to hang, he managed to escape from gaol. Billy was finally tracked down and killed on 14 July 1881 by his old enemy, Sheriff Pat Garrett. He was just 21 years old.

◀ Cherokee Bill killed 13 men in two years. He was hanged at the age of twenty.

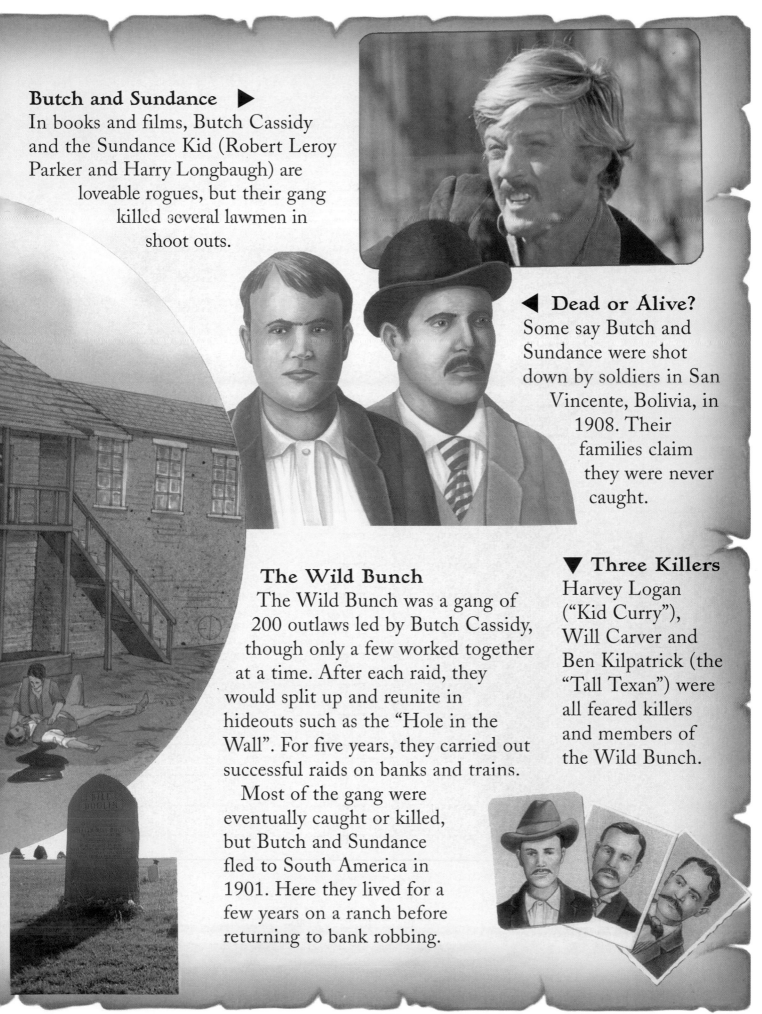

Butch and Sundance ▶
In books and films, Butch Cassidy and the Sundance Kid (Robert Leroy Parker and Harry Longbaugh) are loveable rogues, but their gang killed several lawmen in shoot outs.

◀ **Dead or Alive?**
Some say Butch and Sundance were shot down by soldiers in San Vincente, Bolivia, in 1908. Their families claim they were never caught.

The Wild Bunch
The Wild Bunch was a gang of 200 outlaws led by Butch Cassidy, though only a few worked together at a time. After each raid, they would split up and reunite in hideouts such as the "Hole in the Wall". For five years, they carried out successful raids on banks and trains.

Most of the gang were eventually caught or killed, but Butch and Sundance fled to South America in 1901. Here they lived for a few years on a ranch before returning to bank robbing.

▼ **Three Killers**
Harvey Logan ("Kid Curry"), Will Carver and Ben Kilpatrick (the "Tall Texan") were all feared killers and members of the Wild Bunch.

COWBOYS AND "INDIANS"

In the movies, Native Americans, or "Indians", are a cowboy's enemy. In fact, cowboys were rarely attacked by Native Americans and no cowboy wanted to stir up trouble when driving cattle through Indian territory.

Fierce battles did take place between Native Americans and the US Army in the 1860s and 1870s. Weakened by the destruction of the buffalo herds and wiped out by new diseases brought by settlers, the Plains tribes were gradually rounded up and forced to live on reservations.

Trading with Native Americans

Battle of Little Big Horn

▲ Custer's Last Stand

In 1874, the discovery of gold on a Sioux reservation led to a stampede of miners. When the Sioux refused to sell their land, the US Army moved in, including troops led by Colonel George A. Custer. On 25 June 1876, the Sioux wiped out Custer's men at the Battle of Little Bighorn, but this was the last major victory by Native Americans.

Nat Love

Black Cowboys ▶
Almost one in seven cowboys were black, including rodeo star Nat Love and John Ware, a famous ranch owner in Canada. Another black cowboy, "One Horse Charley", rode with the Shoshone Indians.

John Ware

◀ **Native Cowboys**
Many trail bosses employed Native Americans as cowboys, as they were skilled riders.

◀ While on the trail, cowboys often depended on **Native American traders** for food and supplies.

▲ **"Indians" on TV**
TV shows rarely showed the truth about Native Americans. The Lone Ranger was a popular TV cowboy in the 1950s, but he often treated his Native American partner, Tonto, like a servant.

PART 4: A CHANGING WORLD – THE STAGECOACH

Before the railway, the stagecoach was the only public transport in the Old West. Journeys were long, dusty and very bumpy!

A coach travelled up to 16 hours and 100 km a day, stopping at "stages" along the way to pick up fresh horses.

Stagecoaches were often cramped, with up to 15 passengers jammed in like sardines, some riding up front with the driver or on top with the luggage. There were strict rules on board – smoking, swearing and even snoring were banned.

Stagecoach

▲ Riding "Shotgun"

Stagecoaches are often attacked in movies. In real life, most carried an armed guard who sat next to the driver. He was known as the "shotgun" after the weapon he usually carried.

▼ The Gentleman Bandit

Charles E. Bolles, known as "Black Bart", raided 28 stages without firing a single shot! He also left poems behind in the boxes he'd robbed, signed "PO8".

Pony Express
This fast mail service used a relay team of 80 riders to carry letters over 3,000 km from Missouri to California. Riders changed horses at stations 20 km apart. It took 10 days to complete the route.

Pony Express

Gee Up!
Stagecoaches were pulled by a team of four or eight horses.

Hold-Up
Stagecoaches were an easy target for bandits in the wide open space of the American West. They carried gold, money, mail and other valuables.

In 1877, ex-cowboy Sam Bass robbed seven stagecoaches in just a few months and in just one year, 1881, there were 86 stagecoach hold-ups.

Pearl Hart

Pearl Hart
When Pearl Hart and her friend Joe Boot held up a stagecoach in Arizona in 1899, the driver realised Pearl was a woman even though she wore men's clothes and a mask. Caught by the local sheriff, Pearl got five years in prison, but she became famous.

THE RAILWAY

For over 20 years, cowboys drove herds of cattle from Texas to cowtowns further north, such as Abilene and Kansas City. Here, railways linked the West with Chicago.

By the 1880s, the railways had reached Texas. Cowboys only needed to drive their cattle a few kilometres to the nearest slaughterhouse. The golden age of the cowtowns, and the cowboy, was over.

▼ Tunnels and Bridges

Heavily loaded trains could not climb a steep hill. Hillsides were blasted away and enormous bridges were built to allow train tracks to be laid on level ground.

Across the Continent

In 1861, the United States had only about 50,000 km of railway, all in the East. By 1900, there were 320,000 km of track stretching from the Atlantic coast to the Pacific. The first transcontinental line was finished in 1869.

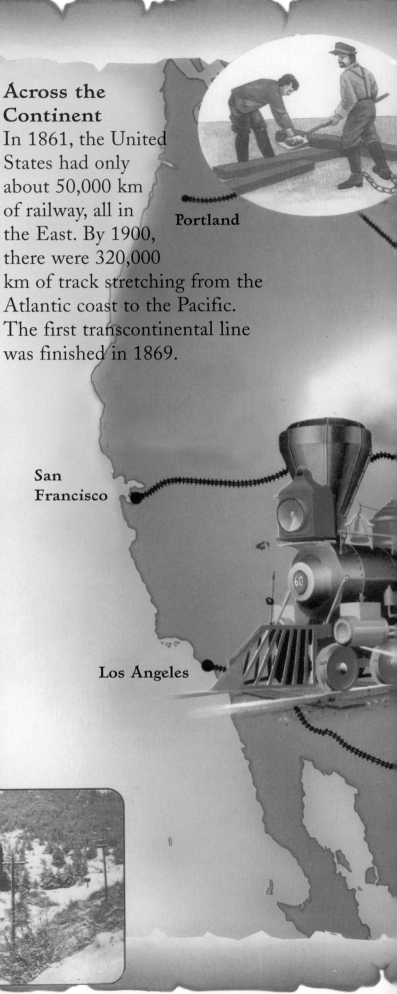

Portland

San Francisco

Los Angeles

Settlers followed the railway. ▶
In 1862, the Homestead Act offered two thirds of a sq km of land to any settler who lived on it and farmed it for five years.

Railway companies told all sorts of lies to lure settlers to the Plains. It worked. By 1900, more than 300,000 sq km had been settled by 600,000 farmers.

Miles City

Bismarck

Minneapolis

Chicago

Laramie

Cheyenne

Ogallata

Omaha

St. Joseph

Denver

Dodge City

Kansas City

Sedalia

Abilene

St. Louis

Newton

Rich Pickings ▼
One of the first train robberies was carried out in 1873 by Jesse James and his gang, who stole $3,000.

Railway Crews
The railways were built by tens of thousands of Irish and Chinese workers. Every kilometre of track needed 250 tonnes of rail and timber.

Dennison

El Paso

Houston

San Antonio

Jesse James

THE END OF THE RANCH?

By the mid 1880s, the cattle boom was over. The price of beef began to fall as there were more cattle than people wanted to buy.

Ranchers and settlers began to fence large areas using barbed-wire. With their herds fenced in and the railway close by, ranchers didn't need cowboys for the round-up. Some farmers chose to raise sheep instead and fights broke out with the cattle owners.

The final straw came in the winter of 1886-87, when heavy snows buried cattle alive or froze them to death. Many ranchers were ruined.

Water pump

Ranchhouse

Barbed-wire

Bunkhouse

Barbed-wire
Farmer Joseph Glidden invented a machine to make barbed-wire in 1874. The steel wire was strong, tough and cheap. It was so popular that within ten years, Glidden's factory was making over 950 km of wire a day.

Winter Work
In winter, cowboys found work on northern ranches. They built fences, and lone cowboys "rode the line", checking the boundaries to make sure no cattle had strayed.

Bunkhouse ▶

On a ranch, cowboys lived in bunkhouses. The wooden buildings were often damp and stank of the sweaty, unwashed cowboys who worked in them.

Bunkhouses were lit by oil lamps and had a kitchen at one end. On winter nights, cowboys played dominoes or braided rope.

Oklahoma! ▼

The musical *Oklahoma!* tells of the fight between sheep farmers and cowboys. The "sheep wars" lasted until the early 1900s, as ranchers battled for control of the prairies.

Barn

Settling Down ▶

Most cowboys retired in their thirties as the cowboy life was so tough. Some used their savings to start their own ranches or farms. Others got married and settled down in towns.

COWBOYS OF THE WORLD

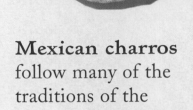

Sombrero

Though the American West was home to the world's most famous cowboys, mounted herdsmen have worked wherever animals graze on open plains, from the pampas of Argentina to the Australian outback.

Until tractors became common in the 1940s, the horse was the farmer's best friend. Even today, there are plenty of cattle ranches around and cowboys are still at work rounding up and branding cattle.

Mexican charros follow many of the traditions of the *vaqueros*, the very first cowboys to herd cattle in America. They still wear the traditional hat, a wide-brimmed sombrero.

Gauchos work on the pampas (plains) of South America. They catch cattle using a bolas, a short rope with weights at each end.

Bolas

Gaucho

◄ Charros

Csikós ►

Ned Kelly

Bushranger Hero ▶
Ned Kelly is Australia's most famous cowboy outlaw, or "bushranger". In October 1878, his gang killed three policemen. Over the next two years they raided several banks before being tracked down by the police. Kelly was hanged in 1880, but became a folk hero.

Csikós cowboys still graze their horses on the Hungarian Plains as they have done for centuries. They are related to the Magyar tribes that settled there a thousand years ago.

Gardians are cowboys from the Camargue region in the south of France, which is famous for its wild white horses and black bulls.

Australian stockmen, or "jackaroos", have used helicopters and motorbikes to herd cattle since the 1960s. But many are returning to the saddle as helicopters make cattle nervous, leading to poor quality beef.

Gardian ▶

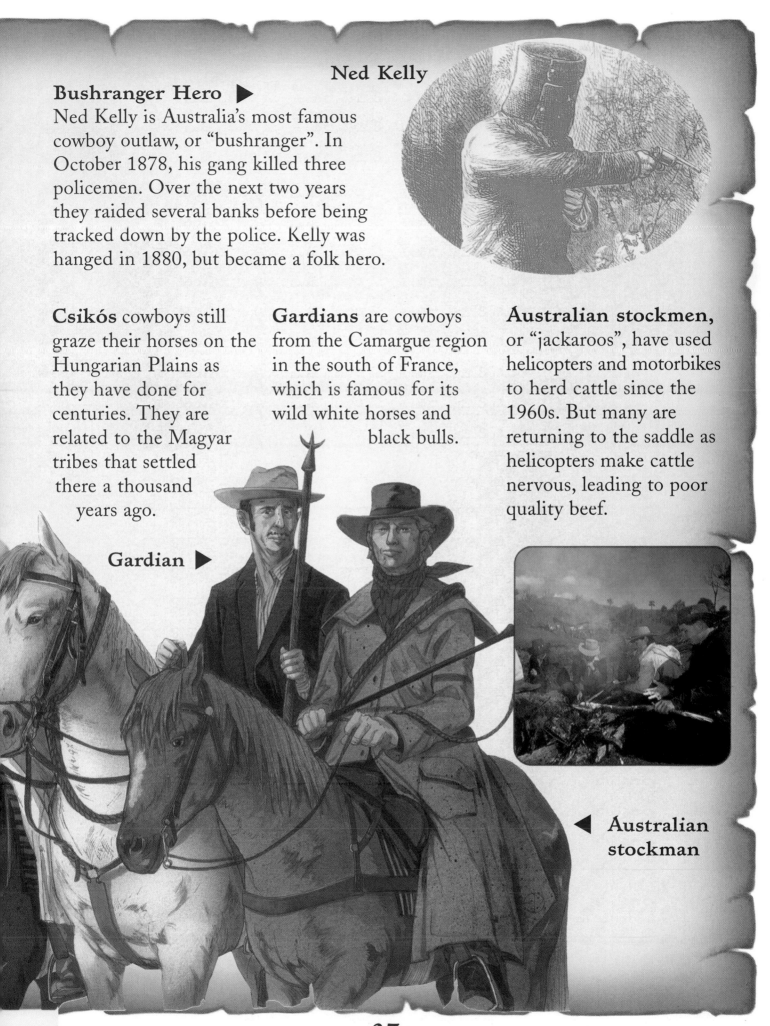

◀ **Australian stockman**

PART 5: THE COWBOY MYTH – THE WILD WEST SHOW

By 1890, the days of the long drive were over. Yet, people were more interested than ever in the cowboys. However, the stories they read were more about shoot outs and bank raids than life on the trail. No one did more to spread the idea of the heroic cowboy than William F. Cody, known as "Buffalo Bill".

In 1883, Cody created his "Wild West" show. Cowboys acted out stagecoach robberies and did riding and shooting stunts. Among the stars were Chief Sitting Bull and Annie Oakley. The show was very popular. No one cared that it was nothing like the real West.

Sitting Bull

Buffalo Bill

Cowboys vs Indians
Buffalo Bill admired the Native Americans, but needed someone to fight his cowboys. Spectacles such as "Custer's Last Stand" made people think that "Indians" were always the bad guys.

▲ Dime novels in the early 1900s exaggerated the bravery and daring of cowboys – but readers loved them.

Buck Taylor ▶
William Levi "Buck" Taylor was a real cowboy, but in his "Wild West" act he rescued helpless women. He created the "heroic" cowboy and made people think cowboys all wore jeans and a stetson.

◀ Nice Shooting! Annie Oakley was a great shot. She could shoot the pips out of playing cards at 30 paces or shoot a cigarette held between her husband's lips.

◀ Annie Oakley
Phoebe Anne Oakley Moses, known as Annie Oakley or "Little Sure Shot", was the star of the Wild West Show for 17 years. In the 1940s, her life was made into the musical "Annie Get Your Gun".

THE WESTERN

Some of the first movies ever made were Westerns. Like the Wild West shows and Dime novels, they showed cowboys as heroes while the villains were always Native Americans, Mexicans or bandits.

TV cowboys in the 1950s were much the same and it was only in the 1960s that films began to show there was more to cowboy life than saloons, shoot outs and hold ups. In recent years, movies have also tried to show Native Americans in a more realistic way.

Tom Mix

The Changing Cowboy

Many Westerns focus on a lone hero who wanders from place to place fighting villains.

During the 1920s, movie cowboys such as Tom Mix were honest men fighting against evil. In the 1930s, "Singing Cowboys" like Gene Autry were very popular.

In the 1950s, John Wayne played rugged gunslingers who lived by their own rules, while the cowboys played by Clint Eastwood in the 1960s were often mysterious "men with no name".

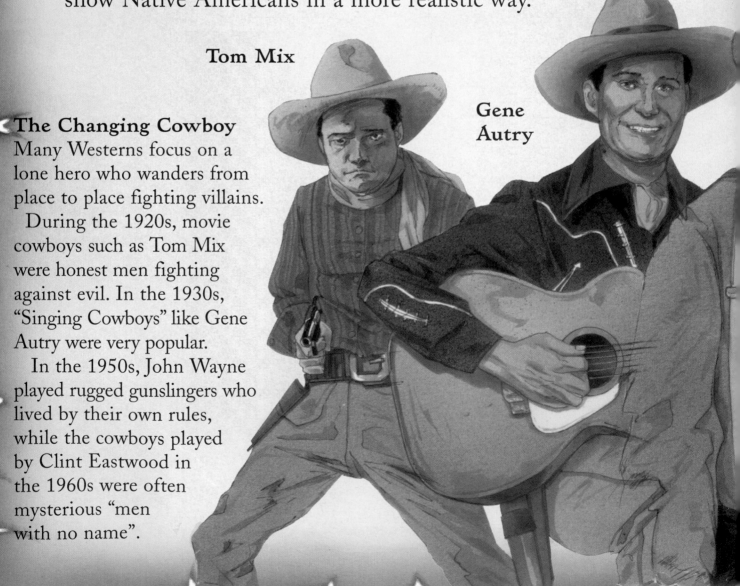

Gene Autry

◀ Comic cowboys
Cowboys also found their way into comic books. Lucky Luke, popular in France during the 1940s, was the cowboy "who could draw faster than his shadow!". More recently, a cowboy named Woody was the hero of the film cartoon *Toy Story*.

▼ Shoot out!
In *High Noon*, one of the great Westerns, a sheriff waits for villains he has sent to gaol to return on the noon train.

John Wayne

Clint Eastwood

▲ Western Scenery
Many Westerns made the most of the spectacular landscape of the Old West, from the Great Plains to the scorching deserts of Arizona. Cowboys are often seen struggling to survive in the desert or battling snow or wild animals in the mountains.

THE RODEO

The round-up was always a chance for cowboys to show off their skills. Later, horse shows sprang up across the West. By the 1900s, rodeos were big business. Today, large crowds still enjoy traditional food and music while watching cowboys compete against each other in events such as bronco riding, steer roping and cattle wrestling.

◀ **Tie-Down Roping**
It takes hours of practice to train for this event. The cowboy has to lasso a calf, then pull it to the ground. Then he ties any three legs with a knot which must hold for at least six seconds.

Saddled Bronco Riding ▶
This is the classic rodeo event which grew out of bronco-busters taming wild horses. Competitors try to avoid falling off the bucking horse for at least eight seconds.

Rodeo Stars ▶

Top competitors can make a living from rodeos but it's hard and dangerous work. Cowboys can be stamped on, crushed or gored by bulls.

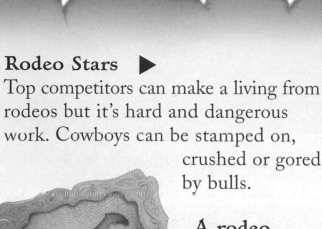

A rodeo belt buckle

Steer Wrestling ▶

Cowboys wrestle a calf to the ground in the quickest time. This event was created by Bill Pickett (1860–1932), who bit the calf's lip to force it down.

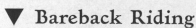

Bill Pickett

Rodeo ▶ clowns

distract angry bulls so that a rider who has fallen off can run to safety. This job takes skill and courage.

▼ Bareback Riding

This is one of the toughest rodeo events. The cowboy has to stay on a madly bucking bronco while holding on with just one hand.

THE COWBOY LIVES ON

People are still fascinated by cowboys and their way of life. Many of us live in dirty, crowded cities and we would love to ride across the open plains or sleep under the stars just like the cowboys of the American West did over 100 years ago.

Even when people don't know much about how cowboys really lived, they want to be like them. They see cowboys as heroes: hard-working, honest, brave and strong. When they wear jeans, cowboy hats and boots they feel a bit like a cowboy themselves.

JR Ewing

◀ **Soap Cowboys**

Cowboys don't only appear in Westerns. In the 1980s, the popular TV soap *Dallas* featured a character named JR Ewing. Though his business was oil, he liked to think he was a cowboy: he lived on a ranch and wore a Stetson and cowboy boots.

Cowboys are still ▶ popular toys.

Dallas

Ronald
Reagan

Acting like a cowboy can win votes!
In the 1880s, Theodore Roosevelt wore
cowboy clothes and held a Colt in
photographs. Ronald Reagan acted in
cowboy films before becoming
president in the 1980s. In recent years,
President George W. Bush liked
people to think he was a cowboy: tough,
straight-talking and ready for action.

"Cowboys" have been used to sell
everything from clothing to cigarettes,
even though
real cowboys
never used
these products.

Cowboy Clothes ▲
Many Americans still like to see
themselves as cowboys. They wear
denim and leather clothes, hats such
as Stetsons and cowboy boots.
Jeans were first worn by
miners rather than
cowboys. In 1873,
Jacob Davis and
Levi Strauss
were the first to
strengthen jeans
using copper
rivets.

Blue jeans

COWBOY WORDS

.45 – Colt .45 revolver.

Bandanna – Cowboy scarf.

Bronco – An untrained horse, from the Spanish word for "wild".

Buckaroo – Texan cowboy.

Buffalo – A bison.

Bunkhouse – A cowboy's home on the ranch.

Chaps – Leggings worn by cowboys (above).

Chuck – Cowboy slang for food.

Great Plains – The level plains of the central United States.

Hollywood – The base of the US film industry, based in Los Angeles.

Indians – Native Americans.

Lariat or lasso – A cowboy's rope.

Long drive – Taking cattle north to the railway towns.

Longhorn – A breed of cattle popular in the Old West.

Long johns – One-piece underwear worn by cowboys.

Maverick – A wild cow or bull.

Nighthawk – A night guard in cowboy camps.

Nymph – Cowboy slang for a woman.

Outlaw – A criminal who is not protected by the law.

Pioneer – An early settler in the Old West.

Railhead – The place where railway tracks stopped.

Ranch – A cattle or sheep farm.

Remuda – A herd of spare horses.

Rodeo – A competition of cowboy skills.

Rustler – A thief who usually steals cattle.

Saloon – A bar.

Stampede – Horses and cattle scattering and running after a sudden fright.

Stetson – A famous cowboy hat.

Stirrup – A foot rest, usually a loop of iron hanging from the saddle.

Vaqueros – Mexican cowboys, the original cattlemen of the West.

Western – A cowboy film set in the Old West.

Winchester – A famous make of rifle.

Wrangler – The cowboy who looked after the horses in the remuda on a long drive.

COWBOY TIMELINE

1493 Columbus brings cattle to America on his second voyage.

1500s Cattle introduced into Mexico by the Spanish.

1700s Almost 100 million buffalo roam the Great Plains at this time.

1800s Spanish ways of handling cattle and ranching are learned by cowboys in the American West, especially in Texas.

1836 Texas declares its independence from Mexico, but many *vaqueros* stay on.

1850–1880 20 million bison killed by hunters.

1860s The first cowboy boots appear!

1860 First mail sent by Pony Express.

1862 The Homestead Act was passed by Congress to encourage settlers to move to the West.

1863 Abolition of slavery.

1864 Start of the Indian Wars.

1865 End of the American Civil War. Beginning of the great cowboy era.

1866 First major trail drive to Sedalia in Missouri.

1867 Railway reaches Abilene, Kansas. Chisholm Trail opens.

1869 Union Pacific Railroad and Central Pacific Railroad meet in Utah.

1870 Ranches spring up in the northern Plains.

1870s Ranchers begin raising European breeds such as the Hereford

1874 Joseph Glidden starts manufacturing barbed wire.

1876 Western Trail opens, after farmers settle beyond Abilene. Sioux ambush Custer at Little Big Horn.

1881 Gustavus Swift invents the refrigerated meat wagon. Billy the Kid is shot by Sheriff Pat Garrett.

1883 Buffalo Bill holds his first Wild West Show.

1886–87 Severe winters kill half the cattle on the northern Plains.

1886 End of the great cowboy era.

1903 The first cowboy film, or Western, *The Great Train Robbery,* is made.

INDEX

Photocredits (*Abbreviations: t – top, m – middle, b – bottom, l – left*).
Front & back cover top, 9t, 30b: United Artists (courtesy Kobal). Front cover bottom, 25m: Universal (courtesy Kobal). 6t, 8-9, 10b, 11, 15, 17 all, 20b, 21tr, 23t, 24, 28m, 32, 33b, 39tl, 47 all: Denver Library, Western History Department. 6m: 20th Century Fox (courtesy Kobal). 7, 37t, 38m, 39tr: Hulton Deutsch. 10t, 12, 13t & ml, 14, 16, 19b, 21m, 22, 23m, 26t, 27 all, 30t, 33t, 34t, 36 all, 37b, 38t, 41t, 42, 43 all, 44t & bl, 45 tr inset, 45mr, 46 all: Frank Spooner Pictures. 13m, 20t, 40, 41b: Ronald Grant Archive. 18, 19t, 35b, 44br: Roger Vlitos. 21t, 25t, 28t, 34b, 38-39: Range Pictures/Bettmann Archive. 25b: Paramount Pictures (courtesy Kobal). 26b, 29m: Western History Collections, University of Oklahoma Library. 29b: Kobal Collection. 35t: Magna Theatre (courtesy Kobal). 41m: Stanley Kramer/United Artists (courtesy Kobal). 45tl: RKO (courtesy Kobal). 45ml: By kind permission of Levis Strauss & Co Commercial "Campfire" with special thanks to photographer Ely Pouget, actor Ethan Brown & Prima management.